Karla Alexander

Quick, Cuddly Quilts

Martingale®
& COMPANY

Dedication

To my brothers, Terry Wilcox and Bruce Wilcox, and sisters, Ruth Hargrave and Shelley Ellis, who always add to my creative endeavors as well as enlighten me with stories about when I was a baby.

Acknowledgments

A special thanks to my editors—Ellen Pahl, Melissa Bryan, and Tina Cook—and the entire Martingale staff.

Baby Wraps: Quick, Cuddly Quilts
© 2008 by Karla Alexander

That Patchwork Place® is an imprint
of Martingale & Company®.

Martingale & Company
20205 144th Ave. NE
Woodinville, WA 98072-8478
www.martingale-pub.com

Printed in China
13 12 11 10 09 08   8 7 6 5 4 3 2 1

Library of Congress Cataloging-in-Publication Data
Library of Congress Control Number: 2007034043

ISBN: 978-1-56477-839-0

Credits

President & CEO **O** Tom Wierzbicki
Publisher **O** Jane Hamada
Editorial Director **O** Mary V. Green
Managing Editor **O** Tina Cook
Technical Editor **O** Ellen Pahl
Copy Editor **O** Melissa Bryan
Design Director **O** Stan Green
Assistant Design Director **O** Regina Girard
Illustrator **O** Laurel Strand
Cover & Text Designer **O** Regina Girard
Photographer **O** Brent Kane

Mission Statement

Dedicated to providing quality products and service to inspire creativity.

Contents

*What better way to welcome a new baby into the world
than with a quilt stitched together with love!*

Most of the quilts in this book are small enough for little ones to carry around but large enough to snuggle with and use as a crib quilt. The quilts are simple and most can easily be completed in a weekend. Personalize the designs and make them unique with your own choices from all the beautiful fabrics available today. Although several of the quilts are designed to be the typical "all-boy" or "all-girl" quilts, you can change the color palette, choose fabrics and appliqué designs that you like best, and you'll have a quilt for a boy who dreams of dragonflies or a girl who may just fly to the moon one day!

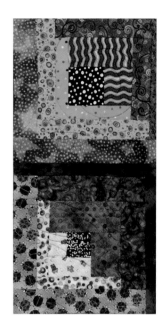

*A sewing machine in good working order,
high-quality supplies and tools, accuracy in stitching,
and a whole lot of passion are the ingredients
in my recipe for a good quilting experience.*

The following basic tools and techniques are necessary to make the quilts in this book. Refer back to this section as necessary.

Tools and Supplies

Rotary cutter. Choose a medium to large rotary cutter. Always start your project with a sharp new blade.

Cutting mat. A mat that measures 18" x 24" is sufficient for cutting the blocks and borders and is a favorite size of mine.

Acrylic rulers. A 6" x 24" ruler is great for cutting fabric into strips. A square ruler is essential for cutting squares and trimming up pieced blocks.

Sewing thread. Use good-quality, 100%-cotton thread for piecing. Match the thread to the general value of the fabrics. I usually use a neutral-colored thread: light, medium, and dark values of tan and gray.

Quilting thread. I use a variety of different threads, from cotton to silky rayon and metallic. Of course, if I send my quilts out to be quilted on a long-arm machine, I let the quilter choose the thread. Either way, always use the best-quality thread available.

Fusible Appliqué

Several projects in this book include designs created with fusible appliqué. I used light-weight fusible web and added a machine buttonhole or straight stitch over the raw edges.

1 Trace each part of the selected appliqué design onto the paper side of the fusible web. Cut roughly around the traced design on the fusible web. Don't cut on the traced lines at this point.

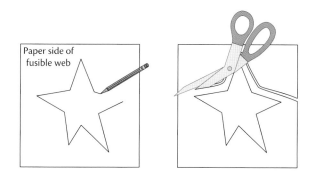

2 Position the roughly cut shape, fusible side down, on the wrong side of the chosen fabric and press, following the manufacturer's directions. Cut out each shape on the drawn lines. Remove the paper backing.

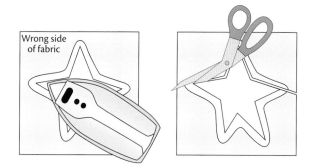

3 Arrange the shapes in the desired positions on the right side of the background fabric. The numbers on the patterns indicate the order of fusing. Use an iron to fuse the shapes in place.

4 Sew around the edges of each appliqué shape using your desired stitch.

Assembling the Quilt

1 Arrange the blocks as shown in the quilt assembly diagram included with each project.

2 Sew the blocks together in rows as directed, matching the seams between the blocks. Press the seams in opposite directions from one row to the next so that seams will butt up against each other when rows are joined. Sew the rows together and press seams all in one direction.

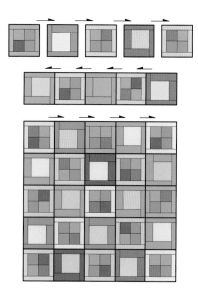

Adding Borders

1 Cut the border strips as directed in the cutting instructions for each quilt.

2 Remove the selvages and sew the strips together into one long continuous strip. Press the seams to one side.

3 Measure the length of the quilt (top to bottom) through the center. Cut two border strips to that measurement. Mark the center of the quilt edges as well as the border strips.

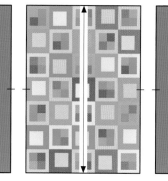

Measure center of quilt,
top to bottom. Mark centers.

4 Pin the border strips in place, matching the ends and center marks. Use a ¼" seam allowance and sew the borders to the quilt top, easing in any fullness. Press seams toward the borders.

5 Measure the width (side to side) of the quilt top through the center, including the borders just added. Cut two border strips to that measurement. Mark the centers as you did before. Pin, sew, and press as described for the side borders.

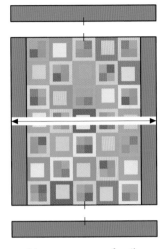

Measure center of quilt,
side to side, including borders.
Mark centers.

Finishing

Once your quilt top is complete, you will need to assemble it into a "quilt sandwich" consisting of the backing, batting, and quilt top. The quilt batting and backing should always be about 4" to 6" larger than the quilt top. Piece the backing, if necessary, by removing the selvages and sewing the pieces together along two long edges. Press the seam to one side.

Layering and Basting

Baste by hand with a needle and thread for hand quilting. Use 1" rustproof safety pins for machine quilting.

1 Spread the backing wrong side up on a flat surface. Anchor it with pins or masking tape.

2 Spread the batting over the backing, smoothing out any wrinkles.

3 Center the quilt top on the batting.

4 For hand quilting, begin in the center and stitch diagonally, corner to corner, taking long stitches. Then baste in a grid, stitching horizontal and vertical rows across the quilt top. Space the rows approximately 6" apart. Finish by stitching all around the quilt perimeter.

If you plan to machine quilt, place pins every 5" to 6" across the quilt top, beginning in the center and working your way to the outer edges. Try to place the pins where they won't interfere with your planned stitching.

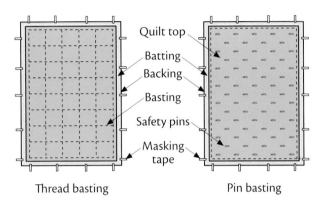

Quilt top
Batting
Backing
Basting
Safety pins
Masking tape

Thread basting   Pin basting

Quilting

Baby quilts are good candidates for machine quilting because the quilting is sturdy and can withstand lots of washing. These quilts are also a nice size on which to practice and perfect your machine quilting if desired. However, hand quilting always makes a quilt special, so choose your preferred method and enjoy the process.

Binding

Binding finishes the edges of your quilt. I prefer a double-fold, straight-grain binding, as it's easy to make and attach, and it's quite durable. I often choose one of the prints I've used in the quilt top for the binding, but sometimes I introduce a new fabric. Since I frequently use busy prints in my quilts, I might choose a coordinating print that reads as a solid from a distance.

1 Trim the batting and backing even with the quilt top.

2 Cut enough binding strips to go around your quilt, as directed in the project. I cut strips 2½" wide for a binding that finishes at about ⅜" wide. Remove the selvages and place the binding strips right sides together as shown. Sew the strips together with diagonal seams to make one long binding strip. Trim the excess fabric, leaving a ¼" seam allowance. Press the seams open to reduce bulk.

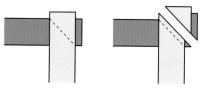

Joining straight-grain strips

3 Fold the strip in half lengthwise, wrong sides together, and press.

4 Beginning about 18" from a corner, place the binding right sides together with the quilt top. Align the raw edges. Leave a 10" tail and use a ¼" seam allowance and a walking foot to sew the binding to the quilt. Stop sewing ¼" from the first corner and carefully backstitch two or three stitches. Clip the thread and remove the quilt from the machine.

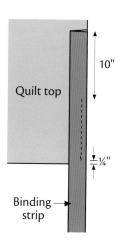

5 Rotate the quilt 90° so that you can work on the next side. Fold the binding up, creating a 45° angle, and then back down even with the second side of the quilt. A little pleat will form at the corner. Resume stitching at the folded edge of the binding as shown.

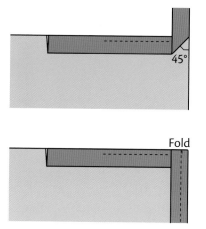

6 Continue stitching the binding to the quilt, turning the corners as described, until your stitching is

approximately 10" from the point where you started. Remove the quilt from the machine.

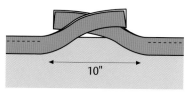

7 Fold back the beginning and ending tails of the binding strips so they meet in the center of the unsewn portion of the quilt edge. Finger-press the folded edges.

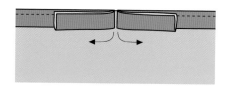

8 Unfold both ends of the binding and match the center points of the two finger-pressed folds, forming an X as shown. Pin and sew the two ends together on the diagonal of the fold lines. Trim the excess binding ¼" from the seam. Finger-press the new seam allowance open and refold the binding. Finish sewing the binding to the quilt.

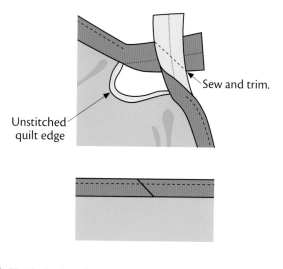

9 Fold the binding over the edge of the quilt to the back, making sure to cover the machine stitching. Hand sew the binding in place, mitering the corners as you go.

Finished Quilt: 36½" x 46½" ❍ **Finished Block:** 5" x 5"

This bright and spunky quilt brings to life the children's nursery rhyme "Hey Diddle Diddle." Artwork was generously provided by William Alexander, my 13-year-old son.

Fabric Factors

Choose whimsical white prints with black accents for the white and black prints, making sure they appear mostly white. Look for tone-on-tone prints for the blue and turquoise prints. For a more feminine version, pair the black and white prints with bright pinks, lavenders, or rosy peach.

Materials

All yardages are based on 42"-wide fabric.

¼ yard *each* of 6 different white and black prints for blocks

¼ yard *each* of 3 different turquoise prints for blocks

¼ yard *each* of 3 different blue prints for blocks

½ yard of blue print for outer border

⅓ yard of medium blue for appliqué background

¼ yard of yellow check for inner border (flat piping)

¼ yard of black-and-white print for appliqué block borders

Scraps (9" x 9" pieces) of black, brown, gold, and white with black for appliqués

Scraps (6" x 6" pieces) of purple, yellow, orange, red, pink, tan, and 3 greens for appliqués

½ yard of fabric for binding

1⅝ yards of fabric for backing*

42" x 52" piece of batting

1½ yards of fusible web

*If your fabric is not at least 42" wide, you will need 2⅝ yards.

Cutting

Cut all strips across the fabric width (cross grain).

From *each* of the 6 turquoise and blue prints, cut:
- 1 strip, 6" x 42"; crosscut into 4 squares, 6" x 6" (24 total)

From *each* of the 6 white and black prints, cut:
- 1 strip, 6" x 42"; crosscut into 4 squares, 6" x 6" (24 total)

From the medium blue, cut:
- 3 squares, 4½" x 4½"
- 1 square, 8½" x 8½"

From the black-and-white print, cut:
- 3 strips, 1½" x 42"; crosscut into:
    - ~ 2 strips, 1½" x 8½"
    - ~ 2 strips, 1½" x 10½"
    - ~ 6 strips, 1½" x 4½"
    - ~ 6 strips, 1½" x 6½"

From the yellow check, cut:
- 4 strips, 1¼" x 42"

From the blue print for outer border, cut:
- 4 strips, 3½" x 42"

From the backing fabric, cut:
- 1 panel, 42" x 52"

From the binding fabric, cut:
- 5 strips, 2½" x 42"

Making the Blocks

1 Arrange the 6" x 6" blue and turquoise squares alternating with the white and black prints into **eight stacks of six each,** right sides up. Each stack should contain a different mix of fabrics. Secure each stack with a safety pin through all layers.

2 Working with one stack at a time, cut through all six layers as shown in the diagram (2½" from the left edge). Take the top layer on the right and place it on the bottom of the stack.

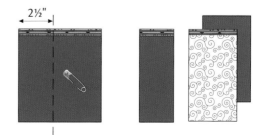

3 Sew the rectangles from the left and right stacks together. Keep the blocks stacked in the same order in which they were sewn. Press seam allowances toward the blue or turquoise.

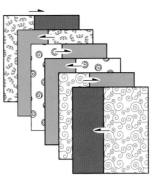

4 Stack the blocks back on top of one another. Measure 2¾" from the top edge and cut through all six layers as shown. Peel the top three layers from the 2¾"-wide stack, and place them on the bottom of the same stack. Each layer should have an assortment of prints.

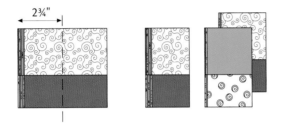

5 Sew the blocks together, matching the center seam allowances. Press seams in one direction.

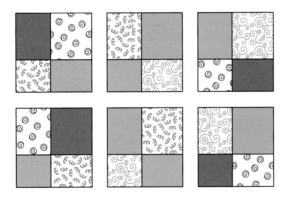

6 Repeat steps 2–5 for each stack to make 48 blocks.

Appliqué

1 Referring to "Fusible Appliqué" on page 4, use the patterns on pages 11 and 12 and the fabric scraps to prepare the appliqués for fusing.

2 Refer to the quilt photo on page 8 to position and fuse the prepared appliqués to the three small and one large blue background squares. Be sure to keep the shapes out of the ¼" seam allowance (with the exception of the hill that is sewn into the seam allowance of the large block). Use your favorite method to stitch around the outer edges of the shapes. I used a machine straight stitch just inside the edges.

3 Use the black-and-white strips to add borders to the appliquéd blocks. Sew the strips to the sides first and press seam allowances away from the block. Use 1½" x 8½" strips for the sides of the large block and 1½" x 4½" strips for the sides of the small blocks. Sew the top and bottom border strips next and press away from the block. Use 1½" x 10½" strips for the large block and 1½" x 6½" strips for the small blocks. The large block should measure 10½" x 10½". Trim the small blocks to measure 5½" x 5½".

Assembling the Quilt Top

1 Arrange the pieced blocks into eight rows of six blocks each. Rotate the blocks so that the blue and turquoise form a secondary four-patch design and identical prints aren't side by side. Remove seven blocks as shown to make room for the appliquéd blocks. Save the extra blocks for the border. Swap or rearrange blocks if needed to achieve a pleasing color and block balance.

2 Sew the blocks into rows and press the seams in opposite directions from row to row.

3 Pin and sew the rows together. Press the seams all in one direction.

Adding Borders

1 Refer to "Adding Borders" on page 5. Sew the four yellow strips together to make one long strip. Repeat with the blue strips for the outer border.

2 Press the yellow strip wrong sides together along the long edge to create a flat piping or "folded" border.

3 Measure the length of the quilt top through the center and cut two folded yellow inner-border strips and two blue outer-border strips to this measurement. Repeat for the top and bottom borders.

4 Using a long machine basting stitch, sew a folded yellow strip to each blue strip along the long edges, with right sides together and raw edges even.

5 Sew the yellow and blue side-border units to the sides of the quilt. Press the narrow border so that it lies flat on top of the blue border.

6 Choose four of the blocks set aside from the quilt layout for the four corner blocks. Trim each one to 3½" x 3½". You will have three extra blocks left over.

7 Add a corner block to the end of each of the remaining borders. Press seams toward the corner blocks.

8 Match raw edges and sew the borders to the top and bottom edges of the quilt. Press the narrow border so that it lies flat on top of the blue border.

Finishing Your Quilt

Refer to "Finishing" on page 6 to layer, baste, quilt, and bind your quilt.

> Patterns are reversed for fusible appliqué and do not include seam allowances.

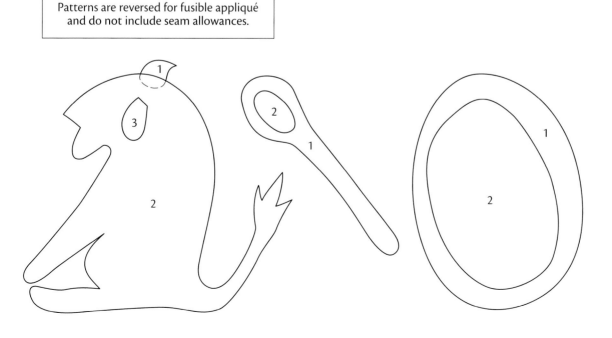

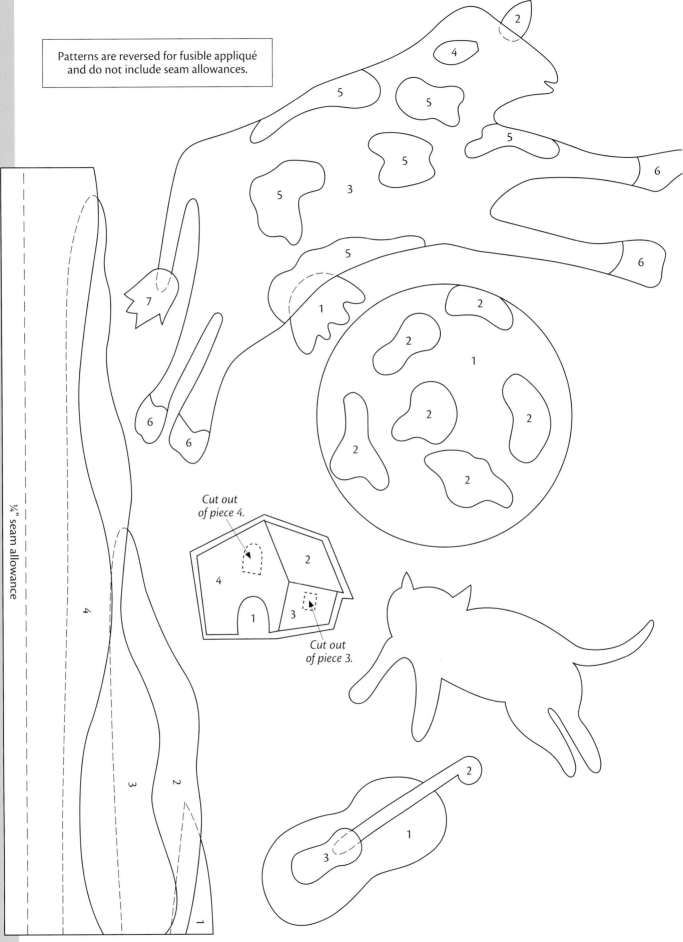

Patterns are reversed for fusible appliqué and do not include seam allowances.

¼" seam allowance

Cut out of piece 4.

Cut out of piece 3.

Machine quilted by SueAnn Suderman.

Finished Quilt: 43" x 52" ⊙ **Finished Blocks:** 5¼" x 3" (A), 3¾" x 3" (B)

After altering a traditional Flying Geese block, I decided the blocks looked more like arrows. I used bright blues and greens for this fast and easy quilt. The machine-quilted feathered vines are a nice complement to the bold, spiky arrow points.

Fabric Factors

Look for a variety of small-scale tone-on-tone prints in medium to dark purples and blues, as well as bright, clear greens that contrast well with the blue and purple. For a softer look, try it in another color palette such as yellows and pinks.

Materials

All yardages are based on 42"-wide fabric.

½ yard *each* of 3 different bright greens for blocks

⅓ yard *each* of 3 different medium blue prints for blocks

⅓ yard *each* of 3 different purple prints for blocks

⅝ yard of blue print for border

⅓ yard of medium blue for sashing

¼ yard of green for sashing

½ yard of fabric for binding

3⅛ yards of fabric for backing

49" x 58" piece of batting

Cutting

Cut all strips across the fabric width (cross grain).

From *each* of the 3 purple prints, cut:
- 2 strips, 4" x 42"; crosscut into a *total* of 8 rectangles, 4" x 5½", and 15 rectangles, 4" x 7"

From *each* of the 3 blue prints, cut:
- 2 strips, 4" x 42"; crosscut into a *total* of 8 rectangles, 4" x 5½", and 15 rectangles, 4" x 7"

From *each* of the 3 bright greens, cut:
- 3 strips, 4" x 42"; crosscut into a *total* of 16 rectangles, 4" x 5½", and 30 rectangles, 4" x 7"

From the medium blue for sashing, cut:
- 6 strips, 1½" x 42"

From the green for sashing, cut:
- 6 strips, 1" x 42"

From the blue print for border, cut:
- 5 strips, 3¾" x 42"

From the backing fabric, cut:
- 2 panels, each approximately 30" x 50"

From the binding fabric, cut:
- 5 strips, 2½" x 42"

Making the Blocks

You'll need to make 60 A blocks and 30 B blocks for this quilt. The rectangles for the A blocks measure 4" x 7"; the rectangles for the B blocks measure 5½" x 4".

1 Pair each of the 30 blue and purple 4" x 7" A rectangles together with a green rectangle, right sides up.

2 Refer to the diagram and cut through both layers of the rectangles as shown.

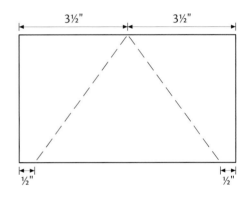

3 Swap the center triangles as shown. Sew the right side onto the center triangle; when aligning the edges, extend the top of the side above the peak of the center triangle to allow enough space for trimming and for a ¼" seam allowance. Press toward the side triangle, and add the other side.

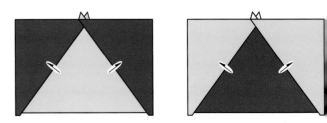

4 Repeat with each set to make 30 green-and-blue A blocks and 30 green-and-purple A blocks. Blocks will measure approximately 6" x 3¾". Trim them to 5¾" x 3½" as shown. Place the ruler so that the 2⅞" line extends through the peak of the center triangle. Leave ¼" above the peak for seam allowance. Trim the top and right sides. Rotate the block and align the trimmed edges with the 5¾" and 3½" lines on the ruler. Trim the remaining two sides. If you are unable to get a full 3½", no worries. Just make sure to trim all A and B blocks to the same length.

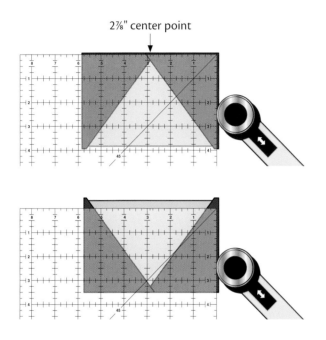

2⅞" center point

5 Repeat the above process with the 5½" x 4" rectangles to make 15 green-and-blue B blocks and 15 green-and-purple B blocks. (You will have two extra blocks.)

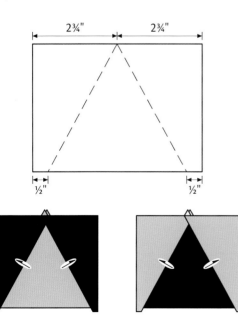

6 The blocks will measure approximately 4½" x 3¾". Trim them to 4¼" x 3½" as shown. Place the ruler so that the 2⅛" line extends through the peak of the center triangle, and leave ¼" for the seam allowance. Trim the top and side, and then rotate and trim to 4¼" x 3½".

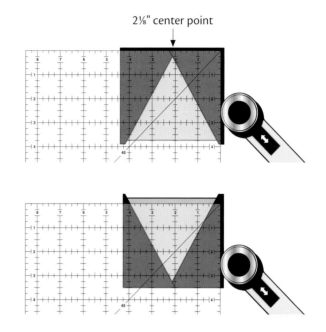

2⅛" center point

Assembling the Quilt Top

1 Arrange the blocks into six vertical rows of 15 blocks each as shown in the diagram, leaving a space between each for the sashing. Position the A blocks in the outer two rows on each side and use the B blocks to make the two rows in the center. The blocks in each row should have the same background value, with background colors alternating from row to row. Once you are satisfied with the layout, sew the blocks together into long rows.

2 Sew the blue sashing strips end to end into one long strip. Repeat with the green strips.

3 Measure the length of a vertical row through the center and cut five strips each of both the blue and green to that measurement. Sew the sashing strips together in pairs and press seams toward the blue.

4 Place the sashing between the rows as shown. Pin and sew the vertical sashing rows and block rows together. Press the seams toward the sashing rows.

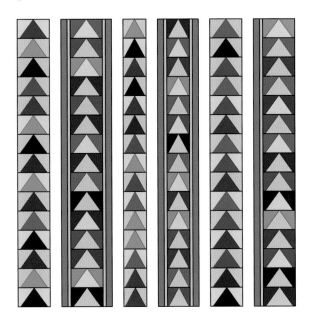

Adding Borders

1 Refer to "Adding Borders" on page 5. Sew the five blue print border strips together to make one long strip.

2 Measure the length of the quilt top and cut two border strips to that measurement. Pin and sew the borders to the sides of the quilt. Add the top and bottom borders in the same fashion. Press the seams toward the border strips.

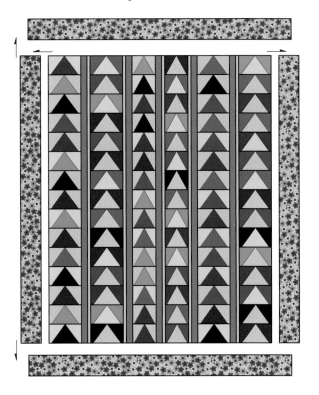

Finishing Your Quilt

Refer to "Finishing" on page 6 to layer, baste, quilt, and bind your quilt.

Both quilts machine quilted
by SueAnn Suderman.

Finished Quilt: 34" x 37½"

With straight seams, strip sets,
and no points to worry about,
this quilt is fast and easy to
make. Customize the quilt with
your choice of appliqués for a
girl or a boy. Both are sweet
and filled with charm. What
more could a baby want?!

Fabric Factors

Small-scale whimsical prints paired with subtle and tone-on-tone prints are a good combination for this quilt. Choose fabrics that are fun and bright, but that also allow the appliqué designs to shine. To make the pink version, substitute pink and peach prints for the blue prints.

Materials

All yardages are based on 42"-wide fabric.

¼ yard *each* of 3 different medium blue prints for blocks

¼ yard *each* of 3 different light blue prints for blocks

¼ yard *each* of 3 different medium green prints for blocks*

⅔ yard of blue print for outer border

¼ yard of green print for inner border (flat piping)

Scraps of assorted red, white, and blue for spaceship

Scraps of assorted green, gold, and blue for earth, moon, and stars

Scraps of assorted pink, green, and brown for dragonflies (for pink quilt)

⅜ yard of fabric for binding

1⅜ yards of fabric for backing

40" x 44" piece of batting

1½ yards of fusible web

3 different fat eighths will also work for the medium green prints

Cutting

Cut all strips across the fabric width (cross grain).

From *each* of the 3 medium blue prints, cut:
- 1 strip, 4" x 42"

From *each* of the 3 light blue prints, cut:
- 1 strip, 4" x 24"

From *each* of the 3 medium green prints, cut:
- 1 strip, 4" x 20"

From the green print for inner border, cut:
- 4 strips, 1¼" x 42"

From the blue print for outer border, cut:
- 4 strips, 5" x 42"

From the backing fabric, cut:
- 1 panel, 40" x 44"

From the binding fabric, cut:
- 4 strips, 2½" x 42"

Assembling the Quilt

1 Arrange and sew the three medium blue 4" strips together along the long edges to create a strip set. Press the seams in one direction. Cut the strip set into eight segments, 3½" wide.

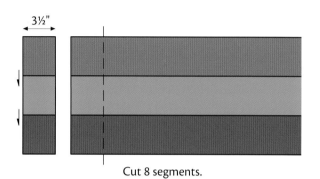

3½"

Cut 8 segments.

2 Arrange and sew together the blue segments *end to end* to form one long strip. Mix up the sections so that identical prints are never side by side. Press the seams in one direction.

3 Separate the long strip into three equal sections of eight blocks each, using a seam ripper to remove stitching where needed.

4 Repeat steps 1–3 using the three light blue 4" strips and cutting the eight strip-set segments 2½" wide.

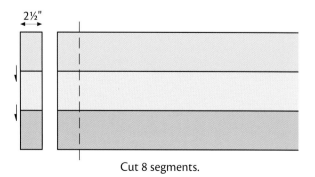

2½"

Cut 8 segments.

5 Repeat steps 1-3 using the three green 4" strips and cutting the eight strip-set segments 1¾" wide.

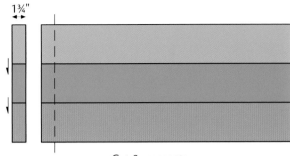

Cut 8 segments.

6 Arrange the vertical rows as shown in the diagram. Position the strips so that the seams will butt together from row to row. Sew the rows together and press seams toward the green strips.

Adding Borders

1 Sew the four green inner-border strips together to make one long strip. Press the strip wrong sides together along the long edge to create the flat piping.

2 Refer to "Adding Borders" on page 5 to measure the length and width of the quilt top through the center; cut four piping strips to these measurements.

3 Aligning the raw edges, sew the flat piping to the sides of the quilt. Add piping to the top and bottom edges in the same fashion. Press the piping flat with the seam toward the outer edge of the quilt top.

4 Sew the four blue outer-border strips together to make one long strip. Referring to "Adding Borders," sew the borders to the quilt.

Appliqué

1 Referring to "Fusible Appliqué" on page 4, use the patterns on pages 20 and 21 and the fabric scraps to prepare the appliqué shapes for fusing. (See page 31 for the dragonfly pattern.)

2 Referring to the quilt photo on page 17, position and fuse the prepared appliqués to the quilt. Use your favorite method to stitch around the outer edges of the shapes. I used a straight stitch just inside the edges on the spaceship and a machine buttonhole stitch for the remaining shapes, including the dragonflies on the pink quilt.

Finishing Your Quilt

Refer to "Finishing" on page 6 to layer, baste, quilt, and bind your quilt.

Patterns are reversed for fusible appliqué
and do not include seam allowances.

*Cut out to make
small star (optional).*

Patterns are reversed for fusible appliqué
and do not include seam allowances.

Baby's Patchwork

Machine quilted by SueAnn Suderman.
Finished Quilt: 30" x 38"
Finished Block: 8" x 8"

This adorable little patchwork quilt sews together so quickly and easily; it includes a simple pieced border made of leftover patchwork squares. The patchwork squares make the design readily adaptable to any color scheme or theme, for a boy or a girl.

Fabric Factors

Choose a color scheme such as blue, yellow, green, or pink. Then choose a variety of six different prints that read well together. Keep your choices balanced by using equal amounts of light and medium values. Have fun choosing—start with sweet pastels or bright prints as your theme. The following instructions are written for the pink version.

Materials

All yardages are based on 42"-wide fabric.

⅓ yard *each* of 6 different pink prints for blocks and outer border

¼ yard of pink print for inner border

⅜ yard of fabric for binding

1⅜ yards of fabric for backing

36" x 44" piece of batting

Cutting

Cut all strips across the fabric width (cross grain).

From *each* of the 6 pink prints for blocks, cut:

○ 1 strip, 4½" x 42"; crosscut into 6 squares, 4½" x 4½" (36 total), and 2 rectangles, 2½" x 4½" (12 total)

○ 1 strip, 2½" x 42"; cut into 2 equal lengths (12 total)

From *each of 4* of the pink prints, cut:

○ 1 square, 1¼" x 1¼" (4 total)*

From the pink print for inner border, cut:

○ 3 strips, 1¼" x 42"*

○ 8 rectangles, 1¼" x 2½"*

The inner border of the blue quilt was cut slightly wider than the inner border of the pink quilt. If you want a wider border, cut the pieces 1½" wide rather than 1¼" wide, and cut the 4 corner squares 1½" x 1½" to match.

From the backing fabric, cut:

○ 1 panel, 36" x 44"

From the binding fabric, cut:

○ 4 strips, 2½" x 42"

Making the Blocks

1 Pair the 12 pink 2½" x 21" strips into six sets, each with different fabrics. Sew each set together along the long edges. Press seams in one direction. Crosscut each strip set into seven segments, 2½" wide, to yield 42 two-patch units.

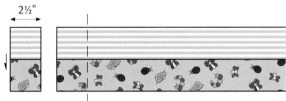
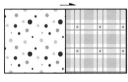

Make 6 strip sets.
Cut 7 segments from each (42 total).

2 Pair together 24 different 4½" x 4½" squares. Sew the pairs right sides together to make 12 large two-patch blocks. Press seams to one side.

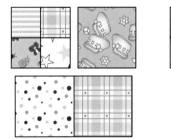

Make 12.

3 Randomly pair the large and small two-patch units and the remaining large squares as shown in the diagram to yield 12 blocks. Two different block arrangements are possible.

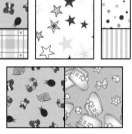

Make 12 total.

Assembling the Quilt Top

1 Arrange the blocks into four horizontal rows of three blocks each. Rearrange and rotate the blocks until you are satisfied with the layout. Sew the blocks

into rows. Press the seams in opposite directions from row to row.

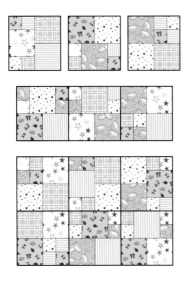

2 Sew the rows together, and press the seams in one direction.

Adding Borders

1 Sew the pink 1¼" border strips together to make one long strip.

2 Measure the quilt top vertically through the center and cut two border strips to this measurement. Repeat, measuring through the horizontal center, and cut two border strips to this length.

3 Sew the side borders to the quilt top, pressing toward the border. Add the pink 1¼" squares to both ends of the top and bottom border strips. Press toward the strips and sew the borders to the quilt.

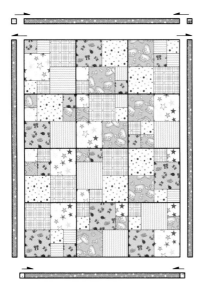

4 Lay out the quilt top and arrange the remaining small two-patch blocks, the 2½" x 4½" rectangles, and the 1½" x 2½" inner-border rectangles around the center of the quilt to make a pieced border. (You will have two extra two-patch blocks.)

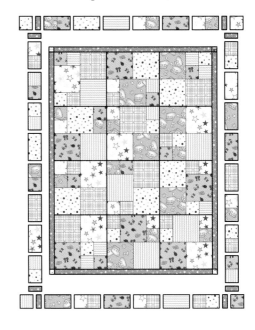

5 Sew the border sections together as shown below. Press the seams in the direction of the arrows in the diagram.

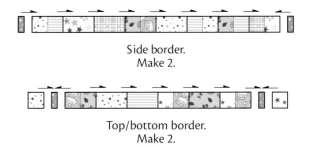

Side border.
Make 2.

Top/bottom border.
Make 2.

6 Sew the pieced borders to the sides of the quilt top, aligning the seams of the pieced border with the seams in the quilt center. Press toward the inner border.

7 Sew the pieced borders to the top and bottom of the quilt top, aligning the seams as before. Press seams toward the inner border.

Finishing Your Quilt

Refer to "Finishing" on page 6 to layer, baste, quilt, and bind your quilt.

Machine quilted by SueAnn Suderman.

Finished Quilt: 35½" x 45½" ○ **Finished Block:** 5" x 5"

This quilt is a collection of framed blocks—some filled with four patches and others with solid squares in an offset frame. There's lots of opportunity to personalize this quilt with fun print fabrics and coordinating color combinations.

Fabric Factors

I chose bright blue and green prints for this quilt with clear bright yellows as a contrast or accent. As a variation, you could choose fabrics based on nursery colors instead. Keep the scale of prints small to medium, and include some tone-on-tone prints. Polka dots are always a good option for baby quilts. Pastels would work well, too.

Materials

All yardages are based on 42"-wide fabric.

¼ yard *each* of 6 different small-scale blue prints for blocks
¼ yard *each* of 3 different small-scale yellow prints for blocks
¼ yard *each* of 3 different small-scale green prints for blocks
⅝ yard of blue print for outer border
¼ yard of purple print for inner border
½ yard of fabric for binding
1⅝ yards of fabric for backing*
42" x 52" piece of batting

**If your fabric is not at least 42" wide, you will need 2⅝ yards.*

Cutting

Cut all strips across the fabric width (cross grain).

From *each* of the 6 blue prints for blocks, cut:

- 1 strip, 2¼" x 42"; cut into 2 equal lengths (12 total)
- 1 strip, 1¾" x 42"; crosscut into 3 pieces, 1¾" x 3½" (18 total), and 3 pieces, 1¾" x 4¾" (18 total)
- 1 strip, 1¼" x 42"; crosscut into 3 pieces, 1¼" x 4¾" (18 total), and 3 pieces, 1¼" x 5½" (18 total)

From *each* of the 3 green prints, cut:

- 2 strips, 1¼" x 42"; crosscut into 6 pieces, 1¼" x 4" (18 total), and 6 pieces, 1¼" x 5½" (18 total)
- 3 squares, 3½" x 3½" (9 total; 1 is extra)

From *each* of the 3 yellow prints, cut:

- 2 strips, 1¼" x 42"; crosscut into 6 pieces, 1¼" x 4" (18 total), and 6 pieces, 1¼" x 5½" (18 total)
- 3 squares, 3½" x 3½" (9 total)

From the purple print, cut:

- 4 strips, 1½" x 42"

From the blue print for outer border, cut:

- 4 strips, 4½" x 42"

From the backing fabric, cut:

- 1 panel, 42"x 52"

From the binding fabric, cut:

- 5 strips, 2½" x 42"

Making the Blocks

1 Pair the 12 blue 2¼" x 21" strips into six sets, each with a different combination of fabrics. Sew together along the long edges. Press seams to one side. Crosscut each set into six segments, 2¼" wide, to yield a total of 36.

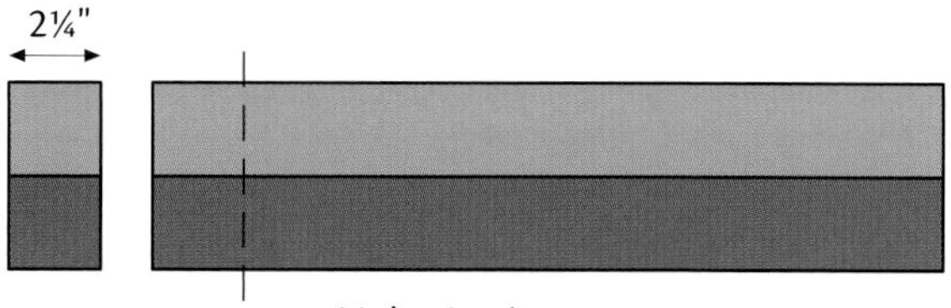

Make 6 strip sets.
Cut 6 segments from each (36 total).

2 Pair and sew together the segments to make 18 Four Patch blocks, arranging them with four different fabrics in each block.

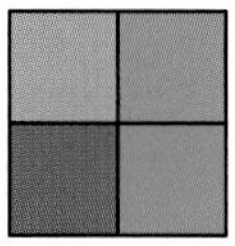

Make 18.

3 Use the green 1¼"-wide pieces to add a border to nine of the Four Patch blocks. Sew the 1¼" x 4" strips to the sides first; press seams toward the border strips. Sew the 1¼" x 5½" strips to the top and bottom of the blocks. Press seams toward the border strips. Repeat using the 1¼" yellow pieces to add borders to the nine remaining Four Patch blocks.

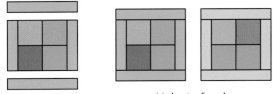

Make 9 of each.

4 Border the nine yellow and eight green 3½" x 3½" squares with the blue strips. Sew the borders clockwise in the following order, starting with the top edge: 1¾" x 3½", 1¾" x 4¾", 1¼" x 4¾", and 1¼" x 5½". (There will be a few border strips left over.)

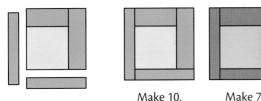

Make 10.   Make 7.

Assembling the Quilt Top

1 Arrange the blocks into seven horizontal rows of five blocks each as shown. Alternate the framed Four Patch blocks with the framed solid blocks. Rotate and rearrange the blocks until you are satisfied with your layout.

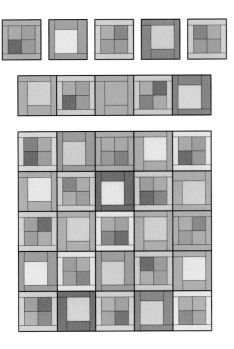

2 Sew the blocks together into rows. Press seams in opposite directions from row to row.

3 Sew the rows together and press the seams in one direction.

Adding Borders

1 Refer to "Adding Borders" on page 5. Sew the four purple 1½"-wide border strips together to make one long strip. Measure, cut, and sew the borders to the quilt. Press the seams toward the borders.

2 Repeat for the blue outer border.

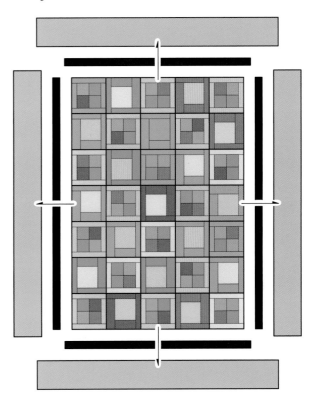

Finishing Your Quilt

Refer to "Finishing" on page 6 to layer, baste, quilt, and bind your quilt.

Machine quilted by SueAnn Suderman.

Finished Quilt: 36" x 45" ⊙ **Finished Block:** 4½" x 4½"

A bouquet of scattered daisies with butterflies and dragonflies flitting about on this quilt creates a fresh spring or summertime look. For a boy, change the color palette to blues and appliqué just the dragonflies, or use the spaceship designs from "Blast Off!" on pages 20 and 21.

Fabric Factors

Materials

All yardages are based on 42"-wide fabric.

⅝ yard of yellow print for Rail Fence blocks and pieced inner border

⅝ yard of medium pink print for outer border

⅜ yard of light green for appliqué background

⅓ yard of pink plaid for Rail Fence blocks and pieced inner border

⅓ yard of pink polka dot for Nine Patch blocks and pieced inner border

¼ yard of yellow stripe for Nine Patch blocks and pieced inner border

¼ yard of green print for middle border

Scraps (approximately 6" x 6" each) of pink, blue, green, and yellow prints for appliqués

½ yard of fabric for binding

1⅝ yards of fabric for backing*

42" x 51" piece of batting

1½ yards of fusible web

If your fabric is not at least 42" wide, you will need 2⅝ yards.

Cutting

Cut all strips across the fabric width (cross grain).

From the yellow stripe, cut:
- 3 strips, 2" x 42"; cut 2 of the strips in half

From the pink polka dot, cut:
- 4 strips, 2" x 42"; cut 2 of the strips in half

From the pink plaid, cut:
- 3 strips, 2" x 42"
- 4 squares, 2" x 2"

From the yellow print, cut:
- 8 strips, 2" x 42"; crosscut 2 of the strips into 14 pieces, 2" x 5"

From the light green, cut:
- 2 strips, 5" x 42"; crosscut into 12 squares, 5" x 5"

From the green print, cut:
- 3 strips, 1½" x 42"

From the pink print for outer border, cut:
- 4 strips, 4½" x 42"

From the backing fabric, cut:
- 1 panel, 42" x 51"

From the binding fabric, cut:
- 5 strips, 2½" x 42"

Making the Blocks

1 Arrange the yellow stripe 2" x 42" strip between the two pink polka dot 2" x 42" strips. Sew the three strips together along the long edges to create a strip set; press seam allowances toward the pink fabric. Make a second, matching strip set using 2" x 21" strips of the same yellow and pink fabrics. Crosscut the strip sets into a total of 22 sections, 2" wide.

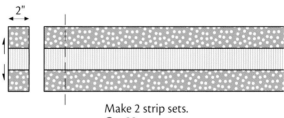

Make 2 strip sets.
Cut 22 segments.

2 Repeat step 1 using one pink polka dot 2" x 21" strip between two yellow stripe 2" x 21" strips. Crosscut the strip set into six segments, 2" wide.

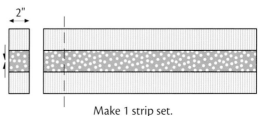

Make 1 strip set.
Cut 6 segments.

3 Arrange and sew together the 2" segments as shown to make six Nine Patch blocks. There will be 10 extra pink-yellow-pink sections; set these aside for the pieced inner border.

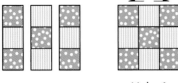

Make 6.

4 Arrange a pink plaid 2" x 42" strip between two yellow print 2" x 42" strips. Sew the three strips together along the long edges to create a strip set. Press seams toward the pink fabric. Make three strip sets. Crosscut the strip sets into 17 segments, 5" wide.

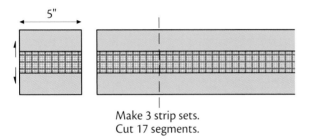

5"

Make 3 strip sets.
Cut 17 segments.

Appliqué

1 Referring to "Fusible Appliqué" on page 4, use the patterns on page 31 and the fabric scraps to prepare the appliqués for fusing.

2 Fuse the shapes onto the light green 5" x 5" squares.

Free-Flying Appliqué

I wanted to let some of the appliqué shapes spill over the edge of the green background squares. To do this, I sewed some blocks together before adding the appliqués.

Assembling the Quilt Top

1 Arrange the blocks into seven horizontal rows of five blocks each.

2 Add the yellow 2" x 5" rectangles, the pink plaid 2" squares, and the leftover strip-set segments that will

make up the pieced inner border.

3 Sew the blocks and border pieces into horizontal rows. Press the seams in opposite directions from row to row.

4 Sew the rows together and press the seam allowances in one direction.

Adding the Borders

1 Refer to "Adding Borders" on page 5. Sew the green 1½"-wide border strips together to make one long strip. Measure, cut, and sew the borders to the quilt. Press the seams toward the borders.

2 Repeat for the pink print outer border.

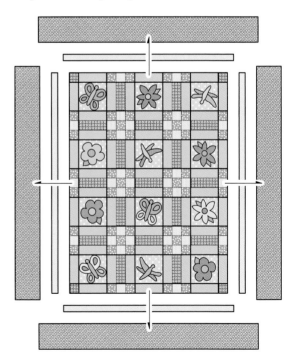

Finishing Your Quilt

Refer to "Finishing" on page 6 to layer, baste, quilt, and bind your quilt.

Patterns are reversed
for fusible appliqué
and do not include
seam allowances.

About the Author

*Karla Alexander, quiltmaker, teacher, and author,
has written three previous books; this is
her fourth book on the art of quiltmaking.*

Karla has also contributed her designs to the popular Martingale
& Company yearly wall calendars and to the book *Creative Quilt
Collection Volume Two.* She has published two single pattern
designs: *Squarin' Around* and *Arboretum.*

She has also created her own design business, Saginaw St.
Quilt Company, which has a line of over 50 different patterns.

Wherever she goes, Karla is constantly observing her sur-
roundings and is inspired with fresh ideas for new quilt designs.
To "keep up the creative flow," she has many quilts in progress at
the same time!

Karla lives in Salem, Oregon, with her husband, Don, and the
youngest of her three sons, William.